Old Age and Young Hearts

Old Age and Young Hearts

Edited by

Judie Rae and Ellen Reynard

© 2023 Judie Rae and Ellen Reynard. All rights reserved.
This material may not be reproduced in any form, published,
reprinted, recorded, performed, broadcast,
rewritten or redistributed without
the explicit permission of Judie Rae and Ellen Reynard.
All such actions are strictly prohibited by law.

Cover design by Shay Culligan

ISBN: 978-1-63980-294-4

Kelsay Books
502 South 1040 East, A-119
American Fork, Utah 84003
Kelsaybooks.com

*To the mothers, grandmothers, aunts, and older women friends
who went before and showed us how to age gracefully,
and who taught us that a sense of humor is essential.*

Acknowledgments

Golden Foothills Press: Thelma Reyna,
   "Grandmother's Insomnia," "On Loan,"

Last Leaves Magazine: Betty Naegele Gundred,
   "A Work of Art"

Levure Litteraire: Judy Bebelaar,
   "That Unstable Object of Desire"

Lighten Up Online: Judie Rae,
   "It Begins With a P"

Page and Spine: Ellen Reynard,
   "I Wonder"

The Rainbow Poems: Ellen Reynard,
   "The Swan"

Rising, Falling, All of Us: Thelma Reyna,
   "To Mercedes in Laredo: an 88-Year-Old Poet"

Stringtown (Finishing Line Press): Judy Bebelaar,
   "Lowpensky Lumber"

Writing for Peace in *Abrazos:* Maija Divine,
   "*Halmeggot,* Granny Flower"

Editors' Preface

The inspiration for *Old Age and Young Hearts* came from a discussion between two poet friends, Judie Rae and Ellen Reynard, regarding the poetry they found themselves writing currently. So much of it revolved around the subject of aging: its delights—retirement, for example—as well as its problems—physical and intellectual issues. Surely, they thought they could not be alone, and so reached out to fellow women poets over sixty for their take on the subject.

As the contributions came in, they read about the many feelings which accompany this final stage of life: the pain of losing lifelong friends and family members, the pathos as well as the hilarity of memory glitches, the appreciation of late-blooming beauty of body and spirit, and joy for the liberation from the need to prove ourselves in this competitive world.

Old Age and Young Hearts is the result of this collaboration.

Contents

Judy Bebelaar
   Lowpensky Lumber   15
   Oh My Moon, Without You I Wept Like a Cloud   16
   That Unstable Object of Desire   17
Greta Broda
   Farewell   19
   I Used to Know That Person   20
   Purgatorio   22
Perissa Busick
   Evening   24
Maija Rhee Devine
   Aging   25
   Halmeggot, Granny Flower   26
Gail Rudd Entrekin
   A Book Before Sleep   27
   A Grandmother's Blessing   28
   Inextricable   29
Mollie Feeney
   Here I Am, Alive Again Today   30
   My Heart Is Not Broken   31
Betty Naegele Gundred
   At the Wedding   32
   A Work of Art   33
   On the Garden Bench   34
Martha Klein Henrickson
   In That Pho   35
   Shifting Time   36
Debra Kiva
   Sequoia   37
Donna Aycock Meares
   A Braiding of Life's Seasons   38
   On the Houseboat in Emerald Cove   39
   Scarlet Leaf   40

Judie Rae
   It Begins with a P   41
   Mid-July   44
   Time Traveler   45

Thelma T. Reyna
   Grandmother's Insomnia   46
   On Loan   47
   To Mercedes in Laredo: An 88-Year-Old Poet   48

Ellen Dooling Reynard
   I Wonder   49
   She Is Finished in Beauty   50
   The Swan   51

Susan Solinsky
   Lost and Found   52
   Reflections   53

Susan Warden
   Lady Admiral's Reverie   55
   Seventy-Sixth Birthday   57

Judy Bebelaar
Lowpensky Lumber

A country song echoes through the warehouse,
cedar and summer dust.
The words unintelligible, but the tempo nostalgia,
melody in the minor key of longing.

At seventeen, I rode with a boy out Refinery Road to Avon,
past the slough, the railroad tracks
or the road through Franklin Canyon,
low-slung oaks tracing desire's deliberate turns,
a September sky holding fall.

Now I sit in this red truck, waiting;
you in the dark loft
draw out the best pieces of Alaskan yellow,
and the slide of wood-on-wood sings too.

We stack the eight quarter-planks
on the rack in rhythm,
and climb in.
I'm old enough to have learned
how things can change in a beat.
In the truck you open the window
to the tune's fading drift
and I slide close.

Judy Bebelaar
Oh My Moon, Without You I Wept Like a Cloud

Quatrain #377; Deman-e Shams Tabrizi
translated by Zara Houshmand
from Turning Rumi *by Salma Aratsu*

Oh my evening sky after just gone sun,
Oh my mockingbirds, long gone from our street.
Oh my apricot tree with fat fruit,
part of the old orchard here,
all the others razed for houses,
did you die of loneliness?

Oh my young husband
who came to me on a sunny spring day,
a strung bow in his hand, a smile in his eyes,
gone these thirty-four years.

Oh how one loss calls forth another.

Judy Bebelaar
That Unstable Object of Desire

In the oldest dreams of old men, women's breasts still remain . . .
medals, emblems of their love.
—Duane Michals

rooms full of breasts
rooms darkened to protect the photographs

a young woman holding her shirt up
with her teeth,
on her head a rhinestone diadem
old breasts, empty, pendulous
cactus bud breasts,
pears as breasts
figs, lemons, persimmons,
breasts over Yosemite Falls

the Arbus waitress at a nudist camp,
hers pert and tanned, her order book
tucked into her apron pocket

I'm remembering nursing Kristy—
that night coming home in the car,
the perfect arc of the Sonoma moon in the sky

I'm thinking of tipis, yurts, hogans, kivas
of California tule houses,
of duomos and geodesic domes

I'm thinking of the crescent scar
on my now slightly smaller right breast,
of the clinical words:
lumpectomy, mastectomy,
of Rachael Carson whose breasts were burned
with an x-ray machine, the treatment that didn't save her life,
of how that little scar saved mine
and how lucky that was

I'm thinking of all the women who get treatment
too late
or not at all

for a while, in that dimly lit gallery in Florence,
I wandered in the world of the breast—
That Unstable Object of Desire

Greta Broda
Farewell

Driving down Highway 49,
a Kate Wolf special on the local radio station.
"Lay me down easy when I die,"
"The golden rolling hills of California . . ."

Then, the warren of houses in Sun City.
My old friend greets me, looking sweet
    with wavy white hair.
I remember her wavy auburn hair
    in 1969 when we were young brides.
It was always possible then to drive or walk over
    to admire a new baby.
We shared neighboring apartments by Lake Michigan,
    flats in San Francisco, cottages in Napa Valley.

After the seven babies were old enough, she finished her B.A.,
and powered through a PhD in Comparative Literature,
becoming Professor Grandma, writing notes on student essays
in tiny, neat penmanship.
Then helping her dying husband with his lungs full of holes,
trying not to trip on oxygen tubes
that snaked through the house.

Today we, both widows now, part ways—I to the east,
she to her daughters in the south.
After we discuss moving—what to leave and what to take,
after she tells me about the 1965 Civil Rights March,
after we remember each of the seven children,
after we eat ginger snaps and pineapple pieces,
I thank her for all that friendship, and drive home,
the rear-view mirror full of the setting sun.

Greta Broda
I Used to Know That Person

The flower girl who tripped and spilled daisies
      on the bride's train.
The third grader who rode her bike home
from the library with a wicker basket full of books.
The Wisconsin girl skating on frozen lagoons and creeks.
The lonely teen memorizing poetry and discovering Mondrian.
The college girl studying Chaucer.
The nurse's aide escorting mental patients to electroshock,
and then going to Freudian analysis after work.

The student living on Robert Street in Toronto,
waiting for Robert to arrive,
her knees trembling, her knees trembling.
The newlywed swimming in the golden dawn waters
of Lake Michigan, returning home with her love
to hear "Lay, Lady, Lay" play on the turntable.

The young woman on Mount Tamalpais on Mozart's birthday
as his minuets issue from a boombox
and a ship is frozen in time on the sparkling ocean.
The LSD caused her to "die" over and over again
on the Dipsea Trail until she let go of fear.

The nurse's aide who cleaned the bottoms of ancient "babies,"
contemplating the truths of sickness, old age, and death
as she spooned mashed potatoes
into their puckered toothless mouths.

The field worker who picked grapes, planted grapes,
grafted grapes, ate grapes,
surrounded by the golden hills of the Napa Valley.

The hitchhiker who thanked the driver and wandered
into the desert to sleep under the vast and unknowable sky.

The Montessori teacher trainee whose home in the foothills
had just burnt to a pile of ash.
The grade-school teacher who taught little children
to read, write, sing, remember the planets, continents,
and the properties of vertebrates.

The homesteader, carrying buckets of water
to heat over a campfire,
as she waited for an octagon to be built of stones and logs.

The retiree driving her sick and confused husband
to appointments and procedures, waking in the moonlight
to rouse him from diabetic comas with spoonsful of glucose.

The widow painting Tibetan *thankgas* and pictures
of flowers, rivers, and galaxies in deep space.

I used to know that person.
Last week I packed her paints and brushes into boxes.
But who is this "I"?
Who is this knower who knew?

Greta Broda
Purgatorio

For my mother on the fourth anniversary of her death

These white socks were yours,
worn now on my feet, that are the same shape as yours,
toes rounded like a fan, the middle—the longest.

Your feet lie in a coffin,
in a cemetery, in Milwaukee.

The coffin, padded with pink satin.
Your body, clothed in pink pants and shirt,
tennis shoes, just as you wished.

In that funeral home, you seemed ready then to rise,
to enter again a discount store,
to push a cart through some vast fluorescent purgatory—
shopping for forgiveness, shopping for mercy,
shopping for peace.

If so, have I been the harsh guard,
blocking the aisle,
accusing you of shoplifting?

Or the clerk,
holding your goods,
refusing you credit?

Was I the robber,
grabbing your parcels, outside in the dark,
shouting that you don't deserve them?

If so, let me instead be your daughter,
discarding my grudge against your grudges,
forgiving you for not forgiving me.

Let me be your daughter,
grateful for the socks,
grateful for the feet.

Helen, take what you need,
then, with a satisfied soul,
go home, go peacefully Helen,
to a peaceful home.

Perissa Busick
Evening

Geese on the pond
swim over reflections
of the tall pines on the clear, still water.

The raven spreads its wings
floating over the top of trees,
so close to the pale, blue sky.

The sound of rain this June night.
The robin dances in the bird bath,
and shakes its wings.

So much to hold and fill my heart,
knowing that soon this beauty
will no longer be seen, nor felt, nor heard.

And what will be
when I no longer
hear, nor feel, nor see?

Maija Rhee Devine
Aging

Do not come running after me too fast.
When time ripens, let's run toward each other,
like lovers under a heaven's smile as when
my first born burst out of me, wearing a crown
of spring rain drops, as when readers, invisible to
authors, lope across oceans, transfuse soul blood, as
centennials take astronauts' puff steps from
the moon into my veins.

Meet me after my long night bus ride over muck-
filled pot holes, wait for me, as my mother did,
bathing in the light from a pharmacy, stumbling
home with me, in my high heels, through a dim
path across a construction site. Let's part the veils
made of my skin shed 7,000 times in my life,
meet like lovers. I'll hold fast to my bosom the jar
of nectar dripped from what consumed me.

Maija Rhee Devine
Halmeggot, Granny Flower

Carmine balsams,
yellow mums, cream moss roses,
and hairy granny flower
crowded our flower bed in our Seoul tile-roof house.

I wish I were sixteen,
Mother said.
That old?
I was five.

I wish I were fifty, Mother said, straightening
her sixty-year-old back while gardening
tomatoes, cucumbers, and peppers in Ohio, my new home.
That old? I was thirty.

Wind blows on my hips, Mother said.
I closed the window.
Wind is still blowing on my hips.
Being a bit grumpy, Ma?

I wore out my heels, bones poke like nails, she said.
I bought her pads, soft shoes,
elevated her feet on pillows.
How does a person wear out heels?

Now at Mother's age,
I bite my tongue not to say, *I wish I were sixteen.*
I pull up the corners of my mouth, keep in,
I wish I were fifty.

I yoga, blow away the wind on my hips.
At a shoe store, I scan for onlookers before I sneak
orthopedic heels
into the shoes I try.

Gail Rudd Entrekin
A Book Before Sleep

Death is a matter of record, a matter of fact, and still
what mystery. Even as you speak your opening farewells,
you want to grab hold of the furniture, refuse the winds
behind you urging you toward the door.
                                                    And yet you are
moving. Things begin to break down and you are
inconvenienced, irate. In time, though, you start
to release your white-knuckled hold on the creation
you call your *self,* allow for the smaller person,
less confident of her shiny shoes, uncertain
about the orientation of her map.
                                          At last
you have to acknowledge your failing belief
that you can keep the books, build the house,
dance the steps. You stay home more,
sticky notes everywhere, reminding you what to do
so you'll remember who you've been, until even that
feels like a book before sleep, and you lie back down,
open your hands, let it all go.

Gail Rudd Entrekin
A Grandmother's Blessing

Thanks for the blossoming trees
in the neighbors' yard that rain pink
in the wind, and for the little girl running,
pausing to pick up petals gathered
by the breeze into piles by the curbs,
and for the way she tosses them up
and the way the petals flutter down
dotting the swirl of her hair.

Thanks for the girl's father, smart
and kind, who was born to his father
and me in the nick of time, and for his father
himself, holding up the roof even now
from his worn armchair in the silence
and the dark with his sinewed arms
his bruised and purpled hands
that caressed the velvet petals
of the dahlias in the park
and took my heart.

Gail Rudd Entrekin
Inextricable

You are the still, solid place to which I return.
You are my safety net when I jump,
my home base when I slide. You are the bed of moss
that cushions me when the horse of my desires
throws me off and runs over the hill.
You are the voice inside my head telling me
to go ahead, and now to stop going ahead.
You show me how it's done, peace,
with your deep quiet.
You keep every promise.
I keep every promise.
Things change and change again.

We are the trees, our arms,
our hair blowing wildly in the wind,
our roots, out of sight, intertwined,
settled in the long, sweet dark.

Mollie Feeney
Here I Am, Alive Again Today

Do I open to the world
of treasures and pleasures,
or do I hide away from
the harsh realities of earthly life?

Where is the inner core that
held firm during past traumas?
Where is the calm breath of hope?
Where is the appreciation of good fortune?

I part the curtains to reveal a world so bright
my senses delight in the exquisite sight.
I absorb the abundant proof of Spring,
and yearn for a halt to cruelty and greed.

Tempered by an understanding that grows
like a weathered oak, I tap into this
hard-earned wisdom. Pausing in the soft
morning light, I step onward into life.

Mollie Feeney
My Heart Is Not Broken

My fifteen-year-old self sat alone in front of the television screen
as the brutal video reported from a country only glimpsed
in a geography textbook. Watching newscasts on school nights,
I saw horrors my teenage brain could not rationalize
and my young heart was unable to assimilate.

Twenty-eight years later, I escorted my mother into a darkened
theater. The film soon revealed scenes in war-torn Europe.
My mother leaned over and whispered that she could not watch.
She was not willing to unearth the pain, fifty years buried.

Now, twenty-seven years later, looking again at the brutal battles,
I witness the shocking scenes of lifeless men, women and children,
killed as they tried to shelter or flee. Horrific images of destroyed
towns, roads, and homes assault both heart and brain.

The silent one, deep inside my core, yearns for simplicity
and peace. But the global conflicts, the local controversies,
the personal challenges continue, on and on.

Have I not earned solace? Have I not paid my dues?
And yet my heart is not broken.
Somehow a strength has carried me safely through my years,
and weathered all these human squalls.

Betty Naegele Gundred
At the Wedding

they rise from their seats
with slow steps or spry,
canes or walkers,
roused by familiar chords

to "Twist and Shout."

The teenage girls snicker
at the old folks
to see white hair aflutter,
sweat on Grandma's brow,
awkward turns,
attempts to twist.

Embarrassing, they think
laughable,
like a funny Shoebox card—
the wrinkled ladies,
flabby arms waving, wide hips swaying,
Grandpa parading across the floor.
How ridiculous they look
dancing like that!

What the girls don't see
are the teenagers, alive
within the aging bodies,
hearts still beating
to rhythms of their youth.

No one outgrows their past

the girls will learn . . .
in time.

Betty Naegele Gundred
A Work of Art

Sunburnt skin and freckles
brand my face at ten.
I scowl at the image
staring back at me.

Skin silken, freckles gone,
cheeks flushed with expectation.
With a flirty wink in the mirror,
I dream of senior prom.

Auburn tresses thick with luster
tousle in the summer breeze.
I have no regrets or worry lines—
tomorrows dance in my eyes.

Carefree, my reflection glows,
joys of a budding family,
laughter lines emerge,
subtle—I barely notice.

Job stress, teenage daughters,
furrows deepen, blemishes appear,
I try more makeup,
add some "conceal-her."

Dim light blurs deep creases,
like an impressionist painting.
With sun light, all is naked.
I cannot deny my age.

Lines sculpted by life's journey
read like a novel across my face—
a work of art, I think,
and there is beauty in that.

Betty Naegele Gundred
On the Garden Bench

Sidestepping to the garden
I cling to the metal rail
gritty from flaking rust.
I used to jog these stairs,
but nagging knees
and wobbly balance
now slow my progress.

Once below, I rest
on the redwood bench,
the one my husband made,
its grain raised from years of weather,
inhale the earthy fragrance of soil.
A gnarled oak casts a shadow—
I see my younger self,
trowel in hand—
dirt under my nails . . .

Blinking back memory, I look up—
robins cheer "good morning."
I smile.

My tulips about to bloom
buds of yellow, purple, pink,
perennial survivors of the garden.
I notice there are fewer back this year
like my life—
more years gone than remain.

Though my age conjures winter,
I prefer to think of spring.

Martha Klein Henrickson
In That Pho

In that Pho on Spadina
watching them sit at a window
it could have been us
they don't know and can't
know   yet
eyes sparkling as they speak
here we sit
we too thought it was forever
not even thought it—
felt it, were sure of it—
f o r e v e r
and here we are without a
f o r e v e r ahead of us
we did not know it then
so swift this time moves
just two old folks
having lunch
with a history that was
a shorter
forever than forever
only now we know this
so many secrets not what
we thought they would be

Martha Klein Henrickson
Shifting Time

Dear departed friends arrive
seen as they were
a span of years
places between them
others from long ago
connecting online
something in me searches and finds them
they remember moments I remember
remind me of what I may have forgotten
we grew up and moved on
cousins from New York to California
an unknown found yet
we share a great grandmother
I keep the thread alive as time shifts
all is shifting
be still
listen and hear the shift
be still
the silence is still.

Debra Kiva
Sequoia

For my grandson, Julian

We lie upon the earth
unafraid of a little dirt beneath us,
your tiny hand enveloped in
mine.

Our eyes soft but wide open
looking up as these
thousand-year-old giants
kiss the sunlit sky.

I do not know what this fierce and wild
world holds for you,
but at this moment
we bask in our astonishment
of these glorious beings,

and there is nothing to do
but love.

Donna Aycock Meares
A Braiding of Life's Seasons

His hand swings mine in springtime.
    My heart swells when we say our vows.
        We share our lives, one bedroom, one car.

His hands hold safe our daughters of summer.
    My heart presses babes to my breast.
        We save and buy our first home.

His hand steadies our walks through autumn.
    My heart's content when he walks by my side.
        We watch our daughters walk the church aisles.

Our hands will clasp at winter's deep slumber.
    Our hearts will rest for we've done our best.
        We'll leave a proud legacy, family strong.

Donna Aycock Meares
On the Houseboat in Emerald Cove

my future
is as blurry as the reflection
in the bay's ripples,
a view
shimmered and shadowed.

How much longer have I,
an egg carton of years?
My old dog ambles aft
coming up to me
as I sit in a deck chair on the stern.
She lays her head in my lap for a pat.
She's eleven now,
but, in human years,
the same age as I.
Her hair is white
around her eyes
soft with contentment.
She still chases dreams
during her daytime naps.

In the water I watch
my grandchildren,
replicas of my youth,
dive, swim, ski,
while I warm in the sun,
pat my dog
and write this poem.

Donna Aycock Meares
Scarlet Leaf

Am I but a leaf of scarlet,
quivering in the autumn air,
flashing hues of fading sunlight
dangling high, without a care?

Do I sense the chill of winter,
deceived by warm October's sun?
Do I catch the thrill of robins
on their migratory run?

Late I wonder what I lived for,
where have all my green days gone?
Had I shaded, had I sheltered,
had I sung, or had I moaned?

Suddenly the breeze excites me,
lifts me, twists me, twirls me round.
Oh, how soft the air delights me
as I flutter earthward bound.

Quiet, I wait for frost's first shudder,
a crystal lacework for my rest.
I curl around a fallen acorn,
hold it snugly to my breast.

Judie Rae
It Begins with a P

You know you're old
when the word you are seeking
eludes you, though you can
recall with crystalline
awareness
the first letter.

For hours
you contemplate
the matter,
watch as the robin
picks berries
off the plant outside
your window.

Poinsettia?
No, that's not it.
It's also not primrose
or petunia.
At 3 A.M. the answer
comes: pyracantha.
Of course.

You know you're old
when the new doctor
you see looks
to be about twelve,
with tattoos revealed beneath
his lab coat and thin shirt.

His hair, dark and unruly,
makes you want to smooth
it down, give him a pat
and send him out the door
the way you fussed
with your son
before school.

You know you're old,
drawing closer to your
warranty expiration date,
and are not fooled even though
the physician eventually declares
you good as new.

What he doesn't say is
good as new for your aging self
with bones that break beneath
the weight of false expectations.

With a brain like a sieve,
you move from actor
to audience, forgetting
your lines, even the simple
ones: the name of the movie,
the book you just read.

Still, there are worse
things, and you can yet honor
the sacred: the bird, the butterfly.

You can still bend—
though not easily—
to catch the fleeting
aroma of the blossom
whose name you've misplaced,
acknowledging, regardless,
it remains as sweet.

Judie Rae
Mid-July

in northern California, and mature
madrone leaves
turn yellow
and quit the trees.

Some green remains,
healthy still, while the old foliage
drop silently, floating to earth
to create a cushion
on the forest floor.

If only we could age
as trees do,
uncomplaining, releasing
our anchors to the skies.

When letting go our hold
of earth's abundance
can we be as graceful,
as silent, as leaves?

Judie Rae
Time Traveler

At ten, I am a yellow afternoon,
a day of blackberry delights
and hopscotch games.
All summer, I
awake to possibility.

I am old now,
a shadow of my
younger self, dodging
grief.

My heart says
bliss, stay here,
shrink sadness,
hide it in my pocket.
Make an altar
of scars.

Thelma T. Reyna
Grandmother's Insomnia

She awaits daylight on the skinny edge of
her daughter's cot, rolled
away in mornings, at night a rusty
sentry in the spidered corner of the hall.
Like a wax figure melting, she sinks to
her knees, now permanently ashed from
prayer, her paper lips whispering the
Credo, Ave Maria, and a hundred holy
lines she can mouth in sleep—if sleep comes—her
knobby fingers twined like vines, wooden rosary
swaying from her palms.

After eighty years, day and night meld into
one. Closeness to eternity makes
blackness deep and long. Her feather body
wafts from room to room, gloom
to gloom, prickly shawl cocooning her from
drafts. She peeks on tiptoes at the sleeping, slumps
beside the stove, flames long-dead, passes to the
parlor, where moonlight cuts long shadows in
the rug and frames her narrow face as
she lifts the curtain from the pane
and peers outside
again.

Thelma T. Reyna
On Loan

Listen, my son, you were never truly *mine*
and I not *yours*.
We've been on loan to one another,
don't you know. All of us are thus: lent
out, like a condo you lease for years and live
in and love and invest in and vacate someday.
Nothing keeps.

My womb was irrevocable house for you, a ghost
umbilicus on you even as I speak. You're so
much in my heart that tears spring
uninvited on the road, at my desk, in my books when
I think of how you've grown
away. Manhood hastens termination.
The lease will end.

At bedside, you swath my hand, put on
your bravest face, recount
your childhood to cheer me with the thought of how
close we've been. The needles do not hurt like
this. For twenty years you've been my sun,
my blue, blue sky, my stars in velvet, my
raison. I may vacate tomorrow, or the next or next.

What giant risks we take! To know
what fluff life is, ephemeral tethers, yet
to bind heart to heart, hanging on, on
loan, on lease, to leave, to lose.
Loss cuts deeply when there's so much love.

Thelma T. Reyna
To Mercedes in Laredo: An 88-Year-Old Poet

You once distilled poetry from cobwebs taut between your
        bougainvillea and the grapes.
Glassene drops shimmied in the morning cool, your
        breathless fingers touching them to anoint your lips.
The tinting of the sky with dawn would draw you,
        moth-like, from your satin quilts, could draw you, naked,
        to your jewel garden, where you hailed rose, camellia, lily,
        hibiscus, gardenia with reverence.
Each day your virgin-eyes relearned the sun, the air, the
        clouds, the slanting of the light in pools of gold
and shadows wet against the trees.

Your books lie quiet now, their songs consigned to dusk
        that clouds your days.
Your hands curl on the rattan chair, fingers stone that
        cannot move a pen or pluck a stem.
Outside, blooms that once inspired paeans curl and fall
        in piles.
Propped on pillows in your window bay, you gaze at
        grandeur that once was, your opalescent eyes
        recalling seasons, reasons, rhymes, and visions.

Ellen Dooling Reynard
I Wonder

My brain is an old house
of too many rooms,
each one more cluttered
than the next with everything
I have ever forgotten, misplaced, lost.

I look in the corner room
for my glasses, but only find
the address book I searched for
yesterday in the blue room.

Next, I try the room behind the kitchen.
No glasses there either, so I peer
into the library, the pantry, my office,
and only when I give up
do I discover
my glasses
in my pocket. I wonder

if each forgotten name,
every misplaced key,
and the mates of all the odd socks
that lie useless in my bureau drawer,
wait for me to fall asleep every night,
then rush gleefully up and down
the stairs and along the hallways,
dash in and out of all the rooms,
then hide exactly where
I last looked for them?

Ellen Dooling Reynard
She Is Finished in Beauty

Inspired by the Navajo Night Chant

Begun from the fusion of two cells in a watery
world, swimming and growing into a living being,
she is born in beauty, perfect in every detail—

from the tiny ovals of her fingernails to eyelashes
curved on rounded cheeks and hands flung
upward in surrender to sleep.

Happy in her sheltered world, she sings, laughs,
and sometimes cries—but only until a giggle
erupts and chases away tears.

A work in progress, she outgrows childhood
to struggle through adolescent pimples
and angst, to emerge at last as an adult.

She gazes at her newborn son and marvels
at the perfection of his tiny fingernails.
As he grows, she continues in beauty.

Middle age dulls some of the glow
until a new sort of loveliness emerges
in her final years, silver hair, glistening eyes.

The day she leaves, the past falls away when
her eyes close with lashes curved on her cheeks
and she surrenders to death's long sleep.

She is finished in beauty.

Ellen Dooling Reynard
The Swan

> *Inspired by video of an old woman with Alzheimer's who remembers dancing Odette in* Swan Lake*: https://www.youtube.com/watch?v=wlAXKJfesBM*

The opening chord of *Swan Lake*
resonates through the room
while an old woman slouches
in her wheelchair, empty-eyed.
Her hands, long tapered fingers,
hang limp and forlorn from her wrists.

An oboe sings the opening melody's
lyric call. The woman's right hand
opens, palm up, then falls, inert, to her lap,
her head droops in dejection.

As the full orchestra swells in crescendo,
the woman looks up and lifts her arms,
fluid grace, sweeping gestures,
hands flutter like feathers in the wind,
head turned in regal profile, eyes alight,
as both arms rise above her head.

Her wings catch the wind current—
the swan is in flight.

Susan Solinsky
Lost and Found

A friend told me she found her keys in the fridge
once. Just once. We laughed. It was
after telling her I found a missing ring in the fridge
on the door, neatly resting on top
of a tidy bag of quinoa. Just once.
But I forgot to tell her
how I danced in the kitchen afterward.

What else is lost along the way:
Friends' names, birthdays, movies, seasons,
then are found hours later unexpectedly
in a parking lot, on a shelf in the cupboard
in a fading photograph or letter.

When someone else lost keys it was amusing
but when I have, there's panic, rummaging
through every pocket, purse, shoe, and car seat
to finally give up
and remember they are sitting
right in front of me. Just waiting.

Susan Solinsky
Reflections

When I go into shops and catch my reflection
briefly in windows or mirrors
then notice what other women are wearing,
especially the fit ones in leggings
and snug jerseys and great shoes,

I collapse a bit, feel old, passé
in my faded cotton shirts and
long sleeve tops stretched out beyond belief
from years of wear and washing
looking like P.J. tops.

I recall my mother in her 80s
wearing the same pale green polyester blouse
over grey or black loose slacks every time I visited.
Once I asked if she had other clothes,
embarrassed again by her choice, knowing how much
she valued style, good fabrics, tailoring and fit.

She'd been a dressmaker during the War
and knew the secrets of seams and buttons.
It was unheard of that she would wear polyester,
a fabric she long distained
when Egyptian cotton, Irish linen, raw silk
and Scottish wool were the best.

She looked down at her melon green blouse
punctuated with neat pearl buttons,
the cuffs rolled up once on her short arms,
and said she didn't think I'd seen it before.

These days, I understand she simply wanted
to look tidy and presentable and I regret not adding
she looked fine and what a good color green was
against her porcelain, unlined skin.
At least she didn't have food stains on it
like some of my clothes,
or cat hairs or missing buttons.

Susan Warden
Lady Admiral's Reverie

I heave to, then pause within a small eddy
near the bank of my existence,
turn my head to search the course of my past.

Many decades ago this infant vessel set forth, sails unfurled,
to emerge from a womb of unlit compact warmth.
Seeing glimpses of what was—mother's smile,
close heart touching,
swinging, or was it flying? skate key on a string around my neck,
garden grazing the peas that earned the reprimand,
"there won't be any left for the family,"
Frosty Freeze ice cream cone, worth a dear ten cents,
Babar and Celeste prancing in my dreams, Christmas magic,
teenage first crush, lifetime friends giggling, a stiff first kiss,
cheerleading, requesting seventeen forever please,
footloose collegiate, full sails ahead with high knots,
sailing too close to the wind, learning the ropes, maiden voyage,
first and only lover, white satin sails filled
with the wind of alliance
and a new dimension of self, cheerful challenging offspring
and their descendants, continually hoisting and dropping anchor,
swashbucklers in many ports, each producing billowing
white sails.
Suffering and delight, tears, fears, sailing with or against the wind,
at times I could not fathom it all.

Turning my head to this horizon here and now
I rock stem to stern as life's rhythm laps at the sides
of my moments with its steady soft song. I swab my decks,
tidy my cabin, gather compasses, locate foul-weather gear.

With the whole nine yards of sail up, I am Lady Admiral, with
firm grip on my helm where I take a vow of continual presence.
I will keep an even keel and give wide berth to harm.
There is only the current of silken wind and liquid life
as my bow cuts the flow with smooth precision.
Sighing with lilting breeze I watch clouds
curl their slow advance at the sky's base.
Voices from the stern bid me Bon Voyage.
From the bow I hear the calling, welcoming me home.

Susan Warden
Seventy-Sixth Birthday

What were all of the moments
of my seventy-six years?
Can I remember
what should be saved, what discarded?
Is any of it hidden from me?
Were there treasures I did not recognize?

The sun always shone on me, birthing newness.
The darkness always obliterated me.
Ebb and flow, it was all regular
like a clock's advancing arms
ticking my life into being.
Here, now, my generous years
reveal a new perspective of it all.

It has always been the eternal quickening,
the cycle that scoops me up
in its exotic arms
like a plump, laughing mother
who kisses my forehead, places her
larger than life hands on my cheeks,
lifts my face, my eyes, to meet hers.

She whispers, "You tasted the nectar of it all.
Wasn't it sweet?
Even now, isn't it all delicious?"

About the Authors

Judy Bebelaar taught in San Francisco public schools for 37 years. Her students won many writing awards; she won awards for her teaching as well. Her prize-winning poetry has been published widely in magazines and anthologies including *The Widows' Handbook* (foreword by Ruth Bader Ginsberg, Kent State University Press). Her chapbook, *Walking Across the Pacific,* was published by Finishing Line Press, 2014. *And Then They Were Gone: Teenagers of Peoples Temple from High School to Jonestown* (2018), written with fellow teacher Ron Cabral, has won ten awards and honors.

Greta Broda grew up in Wisconsin and graduated from the University of Toronto. She lived off the grid in the back woods of northern California with her husband, Robert. She taught grade school for thirty years. Now a widow, she is retired and has returned to Wisconsin.

Perissa Busick grew up in New York City. She spent magical summers in a cabin in New Jersey, living without electricity, running water or indoor plumbing. It was here that her love of nature grew. In the 60s she lived in Paris. Returning to the US, she met and married her husband and had one son. They moved to Nevada City, California where she still resides. After retirement she turned to writing poetry; a morning schedule of meditation, nature walks, and Tai Chi relaxes and opens her to the beauty around her. Her poetry has been published in *Canary Online Magazine.*

Maija Rhee Devine is a Korean-American poet and nonfiction and fiction writer. Her autobiographical novel about Korea, *The Voices of Heaven* (Seoul Selection, Irvine, CA, 2013), won four awards. Her TEDx Talk relaying the book's relevance to today's S. Korean society's critical issues is at: http://youtu.be/GFD-6JFLF5A. She received an NEA Fellowship, 2001. Her works have appeared in *The Kenyon Review*, *North American Review*, in her poetry chapbook, *Long Walks on Short Days*, and in anthologies, including *When the Virus Came Calling: COVID-19 Strikes America*, 2020.

Gail Rudd Entrekin's five books of poems include *Rearrangement of the Invisible* and *Change (Will Do You Good)*, nominated for a Northern California Book Award. Her poems were finalists for the Pablo Neruda Prize, won the Women's National Book Association Prize, and were first runner-up for the Steve Kowit and the Catamaran Poetry Prizes and finalists for the Blue Light and the Frontier Open Prizes. Poetry Editor of Hip Pocket Press, she edits the on-line journal of the environment *Canary* (canarylitmag.org).

Mollie Feeney was born in California, married and raised her children in the Canadian Maritimes. Over the years that she and her husband moved from Canada to Wisconsin and then Illinois, she kept a journal which gradually took on a more spiritual and poetic tone. She currently resides in the Sierra Foothills of California where she writes poetry, enjoys the company of her grandchildren, and indulges her lifelong love of gardening.

Betty Naegele Gundred has enjoyed writing since high school when she was editor of her school's literary magazine, then she taught middle school science for twenty years. Her work has appeared or will soon appear in publications such as *Current, The Heron's Nest, Frogpond, Last Leaves, Months to Years, Orchards Poetry Journal,* and *Open Door Magazine.* Her chapbook *Aperture* was published by Kelsay Books in 2023. She is currently writing a series of memoir stories. Betty lives with her husband in the Sierra Foothills of Northern California and enjoys Zumba, hiking and photography.

Martha Klein Henrickson was born in Brooklyn, New York, and has lived in Canada since 1968 where she has dual citizenship. A visual artist as long as she can remember, she has been writing since she was a teenager. She began writing poetry 30 years ago when a poet friend told her that the notes she had been writing on scraps of paper were poetry and that she should keep on writing. Her poems have been published by *Northern Cardinal Review, Juniper Poetry,* and *Yellow Arrow Publishing.* She has self-published four chapbooks and is currently working on a fifth.

Debra Kiva has been writing poetry as a way to process and honor what life throws at her. She is a certified grief educator and grief movement guide and the co-director of a threshold choir, singing at the bedside of those passing. Debra and her husband recently moved to Whidbey Island, Washington to be close to their grandchildren. She has been published in *Mountain Astrology,* as well as *The Pharos,* the Alpha/Omega/Alpha Honor Medical Society publication.

Donna Aycock Meares is a native of Atlanta, Georgia, currently living with her husband in Grass Valley, California. Having worked as a social worker, she pursued her interests in writing after the birth of her first child. She engages in volunteer work, and enjoys bonsai gardening, genealogy, Zumba, and baking seedy sourdough bread. Donna has been published in *Whisky Blot Literary Journal, Home Life, Romantic Hearts Magazine,* and *THEMA Literary Journal.*

Judie Rae is the author of the novel, *The Haunting of Walter Rabinowitz.* Her poems have appeared in many literary journals and anthologies, among them *Nimrod, Wisconsin Review,* and *Mudfish.* She is the author of two chapbooks, *The Weight of Roses,* and *Howling Down the Moon.* Her essays have appeared in *Tahoe Quarterly, The Sacramento Bee,* as well as online at San Francisco's NPR station, KQED. Judie taught college English classes for twenty-seven years at various colleges throughout California. A Canadian, she now lives in Nevada City, California, a landscape reminiscent of her grandmother's home on the Ottawa River, where Judie spent her childhood summers.

Thelma T. Reyna's books have won 22 national and international literary awards. She has written six books, edited three anthologies featuring about 200 authors, and co-edited the new book, *Doctor Poets and Other Healers* (2022). For over thirty years, her fiction, poetry, and non-fiction have appeared in literary journals, anthologies, textbooks, blogs, and regional media, both in print and online. She served as Poet Laureate in Altadena, California from 2014-2016, and was a Pushcart Nominee in Poetry in 2017. She is founder and Chief Editor of the award-winning *Golden Foothills Press,* based in Pasadena, California.

Ellen Dooling Reynard spent her childhood on a cattle ranch in Jackson, Montana. A one-time editor of *Parabola Magazine,* she is retired and lives in Grass Valley, California. She is the author of two chapbooks, *No Batteries Required* (Yellow Arrow Publishing) and *Double Stream* (South Forty Press). She has been nominated twice for the Pushcart Prize.

Susan Solinsky raised her family in the Sierra Nevada Foothills, on land inhabited by the Northern California Nisenan Tribe for thousands of years. Since childhood, she has painted and drawn, taken photographs, traveled, and written stories and poems about the wonders and heartbreak of life and love. A good, formal education helped hone her creativity. The world continues to inspire and bewilder her as she watches her grandchildren grow into young adults and the land regenerate year after year. Susan has been published in *Canary, Dharma Stream Magazine, Writing for our Lives, Wild Duck Review,* and other publications.

Susan Warden has lived many places throughout her life, each providing a wealth of material for her poems. Early on she taught elementary school, where she discovered the power of story. She became a professional storyteller, sharing fairy tales, legends, and myths with audiences of all ages. Later in life she found herself writing poetry in response to music. She has continued her interest in the art, honing her craft while living in Grass Valley, California. She has been published in *Current Magazine*.

Made in the USA
Columbia, SC
07 April 2025